The Last Works of Frederick G. Kilgour

by Jeffrey Beall

Denver, Colorado

2011

ISBN: 978-146647001-9
First edition.

Cataloging-in-publication data

Beall, Jeffrey.
The last works of Frederick G. Kilgour / by Jeffrey Beall.
Denver, Colo. : [Publisher not identified], 2011. (Library
science series ; no. 1).
ISBN: 978-146647001-9
1. Kilgour, Frederick G., 1914-2006. 2. Keyword searching.
3. Online library catalogs.

The Last Works of Frederick G. Kilgour

CONTENTS

Library science series ; no. 1

1. INTRODUCTION

Frederick G. Kilgour (1914-2006) was a 20th century American librarian famous for starting the OCLC online union catalog (now called WorldCat) in 1971. During the last approximately 15 years of his life, he and his wife lived in a retirement community in Chapel Hill, North Carolina, and he served as Distinguished Research Professor Emeritus at the School of Information and Library Science at the University of North Carolina at Chapel Hill (UNC). During the time he served as professor emeritus at UNC, he continued writing and publishing information science articles, and he taught a seminar every other semester until he finally retired in 2004 [1]. This author was a student in the first of these seminars, which took place in the spring semester, 1990 [2].

According to the Library, Information Science & Technology Abstracts (LISTA) database, all eight of Kilgour's last published works appeared in the *Journal of the American Society for Information Science* (re-titled as the *Journal of the American Society for Information Science and Technology* for his last two papers). Of these eight articles, one he coauthored with Bernard Bayer, one with Barbara B. Moran, and one with Barbara B. Moran and John R. Barden. Mr. Kilgour occasionally gave talks at venues around the United States throughout his life, including during his last years. This author attended one of these talks at the Lamont Library at Harvard University in 1996.

This book seeks to examine Kilgour's last papers, most of which were written on the same topic, to record and analyze what he and his co-authors sought to discover and propound and to place the papers' ideas in the context of Mr. Kilgour's life and accomplishments and to interpret them in the context of the current state of library information technology.

2. THE RESEARCH IN THE PAPERS

All eight of Kilgour's last papers except one deal with the same proposition. Kilgour seeks to experimentally find a way to make cataloging cheaper by inventing a method for achieving precise search results in online catalogs using either title words alone or a combination of title and author words. The papers describe various experiments, all variations on the same theme, that yield a small result set that lists a particular known book a library catalog user is seeking.

In conducting his experiments, Kilgour limits their application to three special circumstances, and he then tries to justify all three limitations using published research. First, tries to establish that scholars chiefly get their information through books. Kilgour cites 1999 data from OCLC that shows that "Requests for books exceeded those for serials by 7%" [3, p. 1204]. Further stretching to make his point, Kilgour cites a 1958 Danish study that found that "monographs, handbooks and compendia were rated as nearly equally useful as journals" [4, p. 51]. Kilgour's statements would not stand up so well today, for the scholarly article now clearly stands as the predominant mode of scholarly communication. But were Kilgour still alive today, I am sure that he would not let this fact get in his way. Interestingly, the ArticleFirst database, an OCLC product, is a table of contents service and not an abstracting/indexing service. That is, it is an article index created with journal table of contents information; its metadata records are brief, and they lack subject metadata and abstracts. Although the ArticleFirst database seems to bear the hallmarks of Kilgour's coordinate search experiments, he had nothing to do with its creation [5].

The next two limitations that Kilgour imposes on his experiments are that the searches must be for a known-item, and must not be a subject search. He and his co-authors argue that subject searching has declined, and known-item searches have become predominant. In their 2000 paper, Kilgour and Moran cite numerous studies, including some their University of North Carolina colleagues conducted, to demonstrate these trends. Specifically, they cite a 1991 study by Ray R. Larson entitled "The Decline of Subject

Searching: Long-Term Trends and Patterns of Index Use in an Online Catalog" that finds that "over the data collection period the known item search percentage has continually risen, and began to exceed the topical search percentage in late 1986" [6, p. 207].

3. COORDINATE SEARCHING

The first generation of online public access catalogs (OPACs) did not allow for keyword searching. That is to say, searchers were limited to left-anchored searches of a single index, such as an author search, a title search, a subject search, etc. There was no "word" searching; the only search results were alphanumerically-sorted browse displays.

Kilgour almost immediately recognized that the addition of keyword search functionality to second-generation OPACs was a big leap forward in online catalog technology, and he sought to experiment with it and to help libraries take full advantage of the innovation. A student of the history of science and technology, he was able to recognize important innovations when they appeared.

Keyword searching here is not the same as full-text searching as we know it today. This new type of searching was limited to searching a single database of online catalog records; it didn't search the full text of books or other documents. Some call this "metadata searching" [7], and most OPACs still offer it. Kilgour notes that keyword searching "was not widely available until the mid-1980s, when the vendors of commercial OPACs began to install so-called keyword searching to their product" [8, p. 87]. This technological novelty offered exciting new possibilities for improving online library catalog searching, and it's no surprise that Kilgour, a proven library innovator, sought to find and exploit those possibilities.

In his last writings, Kilgour refers to keyword searching as "coordinate searching." In fact, one of the last papers [9] is a fascinating history of coordinate searching. The term "coordinate searching" is hardly used today; instead we might just say keyword searching, full-text searching or post-coordinate searching. This type of search looks for words anywhere they appear in a database or metadata record, not just within a specific browse index, and it presents search results that only contain the words entered in the search. Moreover, coordinate searching combines two or more words using the Boolean AND operator, and its appearance in OPACs made possible a whole new method of information retrieval compared to the first generation OPACs.

In his experiments, Kilgour found that when a searcher performs coordinate searching of words from the author's name and the title of a known book by the author, the result set is small, a retrieval that easily allows the searcher to spot and pick out the wanted book and then access it. He refers to these small result sets as "minicats," a word that must be of his own invention and that is no longer used, at least in the library and information science domain. His experiments measure the number of single-screen minicats that his different experiments produce, and his goal was to keep the number below two as much as possible. Kilgour, in fact believed that the minicat *was* the catalog: "Only when it responds to a search request does a catalog come into existence on a computer screen" [8, p. 83].

In his last article, Kilgour writes,

The finding of this sixth experiment that 98.9% of the time a one-screen minicat is produced is important and confirms the hypothesis on page 1203 that "searches using surname plus first and last title words produce one-screen minicats in the area of 98% to nearly 100% of the time." The production of one-screen minicats 98.9% of the time essentially equals the 99.0% of the previous experiment, which also used scholarly citations as data and an identical methodology. Both compare favorably with the revised findings of the third experiment, 96.7%, and the fourth, 98.7% [10, p. 1208].

What was Kilgour really trying to show? He wasn't really trying to invent a new way to make searching more precise; instead, he was trying to show that libraries didn't need to commit so many human resources to cataloging, for his method of retrieval was sufficient for most purposes, and his method could be automated.

His goal was to show that title page information was sufficient for discovery, eliminating the need for trained catalogers and saving libraries lots of money. But to prove the point, two big things needed to be true: the search had to involve a scholar searching for a known item, and that item had to be a book.

Kilgour wasn't shy about expressing his negative feelings towards library cataloging's high cost. Kilgour was among the first librarians to publicly question the value of and need for library cataloging, a trend that continues to this day. [11, 12]. Kilgour may have been the one who initially broke the ice and made it fashionable to question the application of complex content standards to bibliographic description. Not only that, but he also actively sought to prove that cataloging could be minimized. For example, in his 1995 article he states, "The immediate objective of the study is to determine the extent to which cataloging can be reduced ... " [13, p. 704].

Moreover, when speaking of content standards, specifically the *Anglo American cataloguing rules*, Kilgour spared no one:

Advances in computer and computer-related technologies have made possible design of OPACs based on minimal search data that users sometimes possess rather than on the complexities of the widely used 600 pages of the 1988 edition of *Anglo-American Cataloging Rules*, affectionately known as AACR2 [14, p. 146].

Later in the same paper he continues his attack and says, "Cataloging rules and the technology of processing searches should be inverted to fit the data that the user possesses, not the artifact that the user seeks" [14, p. 146].

He had a great confidence that his experiments had found a way to finally reduce cataloging expenditures, and he would continue refining and reporting on his experiments for the next nine years. It's important to note that Kilgour's dispute was with the content standard, AACR2, and not with its carrier, the MARC format.

Perhaps Kilgour's inspiration for these experiments was the special method of title searching that catalogers used in searching the OCLC database, then called the OLUC, or the Online Union Catalog. These searches were called derived title searches, and they were formed using the initial letters of title words. For example, for Kilgour's book *The evolution of the book*, a cataloger would enter *evo,of,th,b*. Kilgour helped invent this method of searching when he was at OCLC and found it advantageous because it reduced the numbers of typographical errors that occurred when catalogers input words' fuller spellings. His early studies also showed that this method yielded small result sets in the OCLC database, but later, as the database increased, OCLC introduced search qualifiers, such as by format and year, to limit search results further.

Six out of the last eight papers Kilgour authored or co-authored report the ongoing refinements to the experiments supporting his fundamental hypothesis – that discovery of known items could be provided to scholars searching academic library OPACs using only author and title keywords. Each paper built on the previous ones, and he incorporated into the later papers the new knowledge that he learned with each variation of his experiment.

With the help of his graduate students, Kilgour and his co-authors used the NOTIS integrated library system at the University of Michigan as their experimental OPAC. There were two things that he learned while using the catalog that led him to re-cast and refine his basic experimental premise. The first was the availability of specific-index keyword searching. "This experiment repeats the overall design of the first experiment but uses a different methodology that was unknown to the author when he carried out the first experiment" [3, p. 1203]. Kilgour learned that the University of Michigan online catalog had the ability to perform keyword author searches and keyword title searches. These two search types increased the precision of his experimental searches, yielding even smaller minicats.

The second thing he learned was that a search that yielded no hits was not necessarily a negative result. Kilgour and Moran [8, p. 88] wrote, "... it must be emphasized that this article stresses that no-hit, known-item searches, as well as absences of hits in displays are accurate responses informing the searcher that the database does not contain the entry sought." Because Kilgour limited his experiments to known books, a no-hit wasn't a search failure but a valuable piece of information: the library doesn't have the book.

4. CITATIONS OF THE PAPERS

Table 1 shows the number of times the papers have been cited, according to the Web of Science database. The 1995 article by Kilgour and Bayer entitled "Scholarly Use of Referenced Information in Physics Journals" [15] is puzzling. It has not been cited anywhere according to the Web of Science, and it is not related to any of the other seven articles in terms of its coverage.

Article title	Times cited (Web of Science)
Cataloging for a Specific Miniature Catalog	2
Effectiveness of Surname-Title-Words Searches by Scholars	15
Scholarly Use of Referenced Information in Physics Journals	0
Origins of Coordinate Searching	7
Retrieval Effectiveness of Surname-Title-Word Searches for Known Items by Academic Library Users	4
Surname Plus Recallable Title Word Searches for Known Items by Scholars	0
Known-Item Online Searches Employed by Scholars Using Surname plus First, or Last, or First and Last Title Words	2
An Experiment Using Coordinate Title Word Searches	1

Table 1: Citations of the papers according to the Web of Science database.

Writing his eight last papers, Kilgour prolifically cited his earlier articles, including one published in 1961, an article he wrote while head of the Yale Medical Library. But because seven of his last eight works are cumulative, he naturally cites the earlier works in the later ones.

5. KILGOUR AS SPEAKER

During his retirement, Mr. Kilgour would occasionally travel and speak at libraries and library events. This author attended an event at which Mr. Kilgour spoke in 1996. The venue was the function room at the Lamont Library at Harvard University, where this author worked at the time. During his talk, Mr. Kilgour mentioned that he had worked in the Circulation Department at the Widener Library, next door, in 1936, immediately upon graduation from Harvard College. He mentioned that it was almost sixty years to the day after he had started working for the College and it was at that job that Kilgour first became familiar with the use of punched cards. They were used to record and retrieve library circulation data. Kilgour had an article published in *Library Journal* [16] about his implementation of the punched card system. Williams summarizes Kilgour's article: "In 1939 Fred W. [sic] Kilgour, general assistant at Harvard College Library, wrote of the implementation of the McBee Keysort system for circulation control, claiming it had reduced annual expenses by $3,500" [17, p. 18]. When he arrived as Professor Emeritus at the University of North Carolina at Chapel Hill, Kilgour was surprised to find that the departmental library at the School of Information and Library Science still used a punched card system for circulation, just like he had done over 55 years earlier.

Mr. Kilgour took the offensive at the talk I attended in 1996. At this time he had published three of his last eight articles [13, 14, 15], and the articles were the first in which he reported his successful experiments with title and author surname keyword searches in the University of Michigan online catalog, a NOTIS integrated library system. He told the audience about his experiments and stated that they proved that we really didn't need cataloging anymore. At that time the Internet had barely appeared, libraries still ruled the information world, and cataloging was the foundation of that world. Catalogers were unaccustomed then to hearing criticisms about the value of and need for cataloging. Today, catalogers are more calloused.

A few brave attendees rose to disagree with Mr. Kilgour, but he shot them down, smiling.

He had his data, and that was all he needed to be sure he was right, I recall. His data trumped their opinions, and he refused to consider any argument that wasn't built on data.

6. PREDICTING THE FUTURE

The unsigned biography of Kilgour that appears in a 2006 issue of the *Journal of Library Administration* cites the 1982 citation he received when the American Library Association awarded him an honorary life membership in 1982. The citation refers to his "voluminous, scholarly, and prophetic writings" [1, p. 564].

The use of the term "prophetic" in the biography is accurate, I think. In his last works, Kilgour makes several statements about ebooks, even though they had not yet appeared, at least as we know them today. Still, he predicted that ebooks would appear, a prediction that has come true. In their 1999 paper, Kilgour, Moran, and Barden wrote:

This series of experiments was originally undertaken looking forward to the day when the majority of books would be electronic with title-page information in digital form and, therefore, possibly subject to computerized "cataloging." It was realized that should such a system be feasible, that processing of electronic books might be anticipated by digitizing printed title pages to be entries in systems similar to present-day OPACs. [18, p. 269].

This prediction, now about twelve years old, is more or less true today. Probably most books published today are included in Google Scholar or Amazon, or similar web properties, and they are easily retrieved using author and title words and without any descriptive cataloging. Even though end users can't directly access all ebooks, their content is frequently fully indexed, providing discovery but not necessarily access. Kilgour was talking about discovery, so his prediction has been fulfilled.

In his 1995 article, Kilgour predicted that "With the advent of electronic books, [the] overall user failure rate will start to approach zero" [14, p. 147]. This prediction is also true. The full-text indexing of electronic books in discovery systems such as SerialsSolutions Summon, and the full-text indexing of scholarly articles in Google Scholar have opened up these texts to detailed indexing never before possible. The minicat system developed by Kilgour has been superseded by relevance ranking, which attempts to limit desired results to the first screen of search results.

He also successfully predicted the use of spell-check software in library discovery interfaces. Writing in 1994, Kilgour said, "OPACs could be programmed to activate an English Language Speller when a reply produced a no-hit, which would communicate directly with the user concerning the finding of the Speller" [14, p. 150].

In library and information science, precision is the proportion of relevant items in a search result to the total number of items in the search result set. Kilgour's experiments basically seek a way to improve search precision in catalog searches, but he never used the word precision to describe his experimental goal.

7. CONCLUSION

Despite Mr. Kilgour's experimental success, his coordinate search, minicat system was never adopted as he envisioned it, and his last papers are fading from our collective memory. He wrote his last works at an inopportune time: the very moment when libraries were passing the torch as the gatekeepers of information to internet search engines. Today, the simple search box has blurred the distinction between known-item and subject searches, and almost every search is a coordinate search.

Mr. Kilgour's minicat experiments did successfully and empirically find a way to generate precise search results, but the conditions required to make the system work – it couldn't be a subject search, it had to be a search for a book, and it had to be a known book – made his findings impractical and impossible to apply in the real and quickly-evolving world of information searching and information retrieval.

His goal to reduce the costs of cataloging using his minicat system, though noble, was not popularly realized. Indeed, many now recognize the need for more granular, standard-adherent, and descriptive metadata. Faceted search systems, in which users narrow search results by selecting bibliographic facets such as format, date of publication, and subject area, only work with rich and precisely-encoded metadata records, records that record every detail of resource description according to established standards.

Published in 2004, two years before his death, Kilgour's last paper completes a record of scholarship that lasted 65 years. The paper ends with an acknowledgment thanking the graduate students who helped conduct the paper's research. But before this acknowledgement, perhaps knowing this was to be his final paper, Fred Kilgour wrote his last published, scholarly sentence: "Much remains to be done" [10, p. 79].

REFERENCES

1. "Biographical Sketch of Frederick G. Kilgour Librarian, Educator, Entrepreneur, 1914-2006." *Journal of Library Administration* 49, no.6 (August, 2009): 561-565.

2. Beall, Jeffrey. "Class with Fred Kilgour." *OCLC Newsletter* 190 (March/April, 1991):13-14.

3. Kilgour, Frederick G. "Known-Item Online Searches Employed by Scholars Using Surname plus First, or Last, or First and Last Title Words." *Journal of the American Society for Information Science* & Technology 52, no. 14 (December 2001): 1203-1209.

4. Törnudd, Elin. "Study on the Use of Scientific Literature and Reference Services by Scandinavian Scientists and Engineers Engaged in Research and Development." In *Proceedings of the International Conference on Scientific Information*, v. 1, 19-75. Washington:

National Academy of Sciences, National Research Council, 1958.

5. Olszewski, Larry. Email to author, Sept. 28, 2011.

6. Larson, Ray R. "The Decline of Subject Searching: Long-Term Trends and Patterns of Index Use in an Online Catalog." *Journal of the American Society for Information Science* 42, no. 3 (April 1991): 197-215.

7. Beall, Jeffrey. "How Google Uses Metadata to Improve Search Results." *The Serials Librarian* 59, no. 1 (July 2010): 40-53.

8. Kilgour, Frederick G., and Moran, Barbara B. "Surname plus Recallable Title Word Searches for Known Items by Scholars." *Journal of the American Society for Information Science* 51, no. 1, (January 2000): 83-89.

9. Kilgour, Frederick G. (1997). "Origins of Coordinate Searching." *Journal of the American Society for Information Science* 48, no. 4 (April 1997): 340-348.

10. Kilgour, Frederick G. (2004). "An Experiment Using Coordinate Title Word Searches." *Journal of the American Society for Information Science* & Technology 55, no. 1 (January 2004): 74-80.

11. Wolverton, Robert E., and Burke, Jane. "The OPAC is Dead: Managing the Virtual Library." *Serials Librarian* 57, no. 3 (October 2009): 247-252.

12. Eden, Brad. "The New User Environment: The End of Technical Services?." *Information Technology & Libraries* 29, no. 2 (June 2010): 93-100.

13. Kilgour, Frederick G. "Cataloging for a Specific Miniature Catalog." *Journal of the American Society for Information Science* 46, no. 9 (October 1995): 704-706.

14. Kilgour, Frederick G. "Effectiveness of Surname-Title-Words Searches by Scholars." *Journal of the American Society for Information Science* 46, no. 2 (March 1995): 146-151.

15. Bayer, Bernard, and Kilgour, Frederick G. "Scholarly Use of Referenced Information in Physics Journals." *Journal of the American Society for Information Science*, 47, no. 2 (February 1996): 170-172.

16. Kilgour, Frederick G. "A New Punched Card for Circulation Records." *Library Journal* 64 (February 15, 1939): 131-133.

17. Williams, Robert V. "The Use of Punched Cards in US Libraries and Documentation Centers, 1936-1965." *IEEE Annals of the History of Computing* 24, no. 2 (April 2002): 16-33.

18. Kilgour, Frederick G., Moran, Barbara. B., and Barden, John R. (1999). "Retrieval Effectiveness of Surname-Title-Word Searches for Known Items by Academic Library Users." *Journal of the American Society for Information Science* 50, no. 3 (March 1999): 265-270.

APPENDIX

The last eight published papers of Frederick G. Kilgour:

Kilgour, Frederick G. (1995a). Cataloging for a Specific Miniature Catalog. *Journal of the American Society for Information Science*, 46(9), 704-706.

Kilgour, Frederick G. (1995b). Effectiveness of Surname-Title-Words Searches by Scholars. *Journal of the American Society for Information Science*, 46(2), 146-151.

Bayer, Bernard, & Kilgour, Frederick G. (1996). Scholarly Use of Referenced Information in Physics Journals. *Journal of the American Society for Information Science*, 47(2), 170-172.

Kilgour, Frederick G. (1997). Origins of Coordinate Searching. *Journal of the American Society for Information Science*, 48(4), 340-348.

Kilgour, Frederick G., Moran, Barbara B., & Barden, John R. (1999). Retrieval Effectiveness of Surname-Title-Word Searches for Known Items by Academic Library Users. *Journal of the*

American Society for Information Science, 50(3), 265-270.

Kilgour, Frederick G., & Moran, Barbara B. (2000). Surname plus Recallable Title Word Searches for Known Items by Scholars. *Journal of the American Society for Information Science*, 51(1), 83-89.

Kilgour, Frederick G. (2001). Known-Item Online Searches Employed by Scholars Using Surname plus First, or Last, or First and Last Title Words. *Journal of the American Society for Information Science* & Technology, 52(14), 1203-1209.

Kilgour, Frederick G. (2004). An Experiment Using Coordinate Title Word Searches. *Journal of the American Society for Information Science* & Technology, 55(1), 74-80.

Jeffrey Beall

ABOUT THE AUTHOR

Jeffrey Beall is a metadata librarian at Auraria Library, University of Colorado Denver.

Jeffrey Beall